A NEWFOUNDLAND
Journal

Janet MacFadyen
poetry

*for Bob Creed
and L'Anse aux Meadows
Shutesbury
10/19/09
[signature]*

A NEWFOUNDLAND
Journal

Janet MacFadyen
poetry

killick press
an imprint of Creative Publishers

St. John's, Newfoundland and Labrador
2009

© 2009, Janet MacFadyen

 Canada Council **Conseil des Arts**
for the Arts **du Canada**

We gratefully acknowledge the financial support of the Canada Council for
the Arts, the Government of Canada through the Book Publishing Industry
Development Program (BPIDP), and the Government of Newfoundland and
Labrador through the Department of Tourism, Culture and Recreation for our
publishing program.

Cover Design by Todd Manning
Cover Photo by Stephen Schmidt
Layout by Joanne Snook-Hann
Printed on acid-free paper

Published by
CREATIVE PUBLISHERS
an imprint of CREATIVE BOOK PUBLISHING
a Transcontinental Inc. associated company
P.O. Box 8660, Stn. A
St. John's, Newfoundland and Labrador A1B 3T7

Printed in Canada by:
TRANSCONTINENTAL INC.

Library and Archives Canada Cataloguing in Publication

MacFadyen, Janet
A Newfoundland journal / by Janet MacFadyen.

Poems.
ISBN 978-1-897174-37-1

1. Newfoundland and Labrador--Poetry. I. Title.

PS3613.A34N49 2009   811'.6   C2009-900398-8

for Steve

Who knows why we were there.
We had visions
of the long gray arms of the sea,
of places where we could not predict
how the road turned or the wind blew.

The Vikings
found a home at L'Anse aux Meadows
where others even earlier
hunted whales and seals and fish.
But little in that blowing tundra
felt like home, and I knew nothing
  of fishing because my life depended on it.

*

At Port aux Basques, near Isle aux Morts,
we belched forth from the belly of the whale:
sardine-packed tractor trailers, pop-up campers,
Tiogas, Discoveries, Pace Arrows, and untold
numbers of four-wheeled mosquitoes
including our van.
  Across Red Rock and the Wreckhouse,
by Table, Steel, and Marble mountains,
Seal Rock, Flat Bay, Blow-Me-Down,
Sally's Cove, Cow Head,
River of Ponds and Port aux Choix,
and the ferry to Labrador at St. Barbe;
past the white spare houses of Deadman's Cove,
Flower's Cove, Nameless Cove glinting by a cobalt sea
and the long
lazy curve around the final point
where everything came to a halt
       at Wild Bight and Cape Onion.

*

There it was
only eleven miles across the Strait.
I know people who have been to Labrador,
who have seen up close
those white houses, maroon cliffs
and who knows what else,
a story of shipwreck and Basque whalers
and a road that soon turns to gravel and peters out.
Then the only way forward is by ferry
            into a land
of "intolerable fog and ice."

We gazed across that bluest water
                    and turned around.

Saturday

I thought Gros Morne meant "Big Morning"
referring to the dawn—
But I would have come here anyway
had I known the truth: it is
Head in the Clouds, the Big Gloomy, Cheerless, Forlorn.
    When people say the island's name
the *found* is lost.
Everything hinges on the last syllable—New-f'n-LAND:
home port, lobster pots stacked,
the high-bowed, wide-beamed boats
on scaffolding, curtains drawn
in a fisherman's cottage
    fifty feet from the rolling surf.

    At Lobster Cove Lighthouse, semaphore flags
snap in the wind. We go down
past the white curved steel to a door.
Inside: a wall of old photographs,
men and ice, and a life you could reach
only by boat, codfish drying
on racks of rope. At dusk
light shines a warning over the rocks;
  by day the flags relay a single word
        to passing boats:
            bottomer.

Emerging from a bank of fog
        we drifted
    into the Visitor Centre,
learned the name of mustardy rocks,
learned and just as quickly forgot.

Where had we been, except
cloaked valleys, curtains of rain?
The whole of Newfoundland lay under a veil,
    her long hair
        draping down to the sea:
the sailor's wife waiting for the ship's return,
the fishermen waiting for the fish.

A gray sea and a blue shore.
A small white house on a rocky coast.
And thousands of shipwrecks,
sailors blown off course like Bjarni Herjolfsson
whose longboat churned westward in a storm,
and when the seas subsided
he caught a glimpse of something hazy
    on the horizon, something
                unrecorded.

      *

Clouds—
you can almost see the tops
of the Long Range Mountains.
The mind
reaches its fingers around an idea,
the tide
grasps a sand bar, tentatively at first, then assertively.
A new tool, a new approach:
the way around the island is by boat, not by road,
the way around the rock is by water.
Oh, slowly wonder reveals itself to the world.
    Oh, so very slowly
what I wanted
      vanished on the ocean.

      *

A slender
    blue finger of sky to the west.
Will it peel back the clouds
from the top of that mountain,
and let me lay eyes on it?

Look, a procession of cliffs
and the hovering clouds about to lift:
someone tugging at the bedcovers to see
      who is under there.

All day the world
has been a low bank of clouds rolling away towards the east,
                    and now the sun breaks through.

    What's next?
Will we see the next town, the next bay?
When we wake, where shall we find ourselves,
in what room, what country?
It is never the same from valley to valley,
night to night.
We rise in the morning to see land take form
one cliff and bay at a time,
one mountain after another:
    Big Level, Old Crow, Big Lookout, Gros Morne.

            *

    At Green Point someone has gone to work
with pinking shears. The cliffs are trimmed
with rows of rickrack,
            scalloped ribbons on a girl's dress—
It's a ragged cardiograph, the lives
of billions of creatures, long extinct,
where line after line
                on the delicate page of rock
        has been read by paleontologists.

            A sudden shift

                                the long

repeated pattern strung out across the cliffs
is broken, the riff
            abruptly stops.

    Tide
creeps around the rock-strewn point.
A cormorant dries its wings. The sun
is streaming behind the clouds.

A seagull rises,
something dark clamped in its beak,
hovers, then lets it drop—

    pile of broken shells,
        clumped mussels
            waiting for the water. The point
has not yet disappeared.

A pelting rain begins.
Dark cliffs are hatched with gray:
a series of dashes on a page—

and then
          a breathlessness

    *

       a cormorant

          stretches out its wings at the end of the point
     only bright spot of sky
directly behind   small dark figure
against the incoming tide

Sunday

In an alpine meadow near the tree line,
flowers of the pitcher plants
curl over tiny oceans
where insects struggle to stay afloat.
Crimson plants with swollen pods,
                        black flies gathering—

We are sitting on this boardwalk listening
to the moving sheet of water underneath.

We thought   this would be a shorter climb
    we thought
        it would be faster
    before we were lulled by voices
calling from the bog

            quiet movement of blowing grass, the leaves
of something that could be sheep laurel

        *

    The pitcher plants are ringed
 with firs bent double from the wind
branches corkscrewed and half dead,
silvered, stunted—
Whole mats of tuckamore face windward,
a quickened net of branches
too thick to cut through, too thick
even for the wind.
    You can stop and rest in the lee of them
        and be comforted.

        *

    A stairway winds its way
to the summit, a stairway and a boardwalk,
through tangles and the bog
around fog and castled stones.
On the other side—blueberries,
grasses burning with the autumn—
    we sit down
            and forget...

Great cauldron across the valley:
the Tablelands steam with clouds,
   the Tablelands are boiling,
    scratchy orange stone,
     useless water, heavy
with nickel, iron, manganese, chromium.

    *

Earth's mantle pushed up & out   brick-colored
flat-topped: peridotite w/serpentine, olivine & pyroxene—

    *

Table Mountain, Triangle Mountain,
trapezoid and rhombus:
someone with a geometric frame of mind
must have made this place, someone
with a love of Euclid and trisected angles
who took a compass and sheet of paper
to give the precipices and the gravel
   internal order and outer form.
     If you were to draw an arc
   down from the summit of the Tablelands
across the road that divides the valley
and up the other side,
you would find yourself where we are now:
on a narrow mountain boardwalk
   listening
        to unseen water flowing down.

Blueberry bushes. A cloud like a lozenge.

    *

The flanks of old Tableland are in a dripping cloud
and then that bowl,
half a stupendous ashtray,
collects the clouds which belly out and downward—
Some unseen ceiling keeps them low, sheets
   pressed under a steam iron.

12

An old road
in a valley of boulders,
a valley with a black river flowing down
from the distant high headwall and patch of snow.
Between orange stones you find the occasional
purple campanula
laying a single bell against the ground.
I have to catch myself not to step on them,
so delicate and invisible.

The tracks vanish at the river; you can make out
a footpath continuing on, increasingly haphazard
then disappearing.
If we were true adventurers, the foot
would find its way around the rocks
and the hand
would seek out corner and crevice in the boulders
until the trail unfolded before our eyes
miraculously in the wilderness.

Branches stream across the ground
a prostrate dwarf spruce.

You would think it's dead but then you see
a few green needles—
I can follow
the silvered branches over and under the stones,
seeking a roothold in the cracks
like a rock climber.
It's alive and probably older than I am
if the guide I have is to be believed.

So many
abandoned branches.

*

Here's a blue-green stone, iridescence
    rippling across its surface.
        Along the black river
tiny colonnades of crystals:
wash of calcium, vein of quartz,
        milky white.

    I have a geologic map
with bands of salmon, pumpkin, lime and aquamarine,
a map with vegetation and topography
in two languages, footnotes and a key.
    And so you can tell that heath-lichen tundra
clings to "bedrock primarily of diabase"
and sphagnum bogs love
    the blue-and-yellow stripes of ancient seabeds.

    Everything has a bond
to what lays close, the way
two people next to each other
discover an affection, even
when there was no intent.

A deepening flush, the wind pauses,
every living thing takes a breath—
You would hear the high note of some unknown bird now,
    if there were birds that lived
        in the plantless bugless barrens
            only

            there are not.

Monday

Once there was a man
who set out to canoe to Ungava Bay.
I don't know if he put in at Happy Valley or Nain,
but his route followed unnamed rivers,
countless valleys, and in October
with the fall in flames
he turned round to retrace his voyage.
    Then he found himself
in a landscape where every mountain looked the same,
the fork in every river seemed familiar
but only one led home.
And so he remained in that place,
        he willed his body to it.

    I wonder
how many people drive off the ferry at Blanc Sablon
with the Triple A map on their laps
only to find the pavement stops
at the Basque whaling station at Red Bay,
the road to Cartwright is two hundred miles of gravel,
and the long white route across the page
is a snowmobile track.

I was afraid of the wind.
I was afraid to leave the land in the wind.
I was afraid
of a place with only sixty miles of pavement and no way back
except by water, to go one last measure past
what my heart told me I was able,
even if it was only another road,
        another ferry   another distant shore,
                and many others had gone before me.

        *

Past Flower's Cove   where her mother sewed sealskin
boots, dogsleds for wood & water, the way out by boat
easier   than hacking your way through tuckamore…

"We never knew how beautiful this land was until the road came through."

*

A campground somewhere in a piney forest,
north of Maine and east of Labrador, with a small
lake and a skiff, a half dozen people and two ducks,
two park rangers eating tomatoes and rice,
a government sign about boiling water,
    the moon and Mars and a stippling of cloud.

I wish I could say
we watched the Northern Lights that night,
that millions of stars swung from the polestar to the horizon.
But the air was raw and it started to rain;
we got into sleeping bags,
the tent oozed overhead
        and I dreamed.

Tuesday

He had spent his boyhood around the grassy mounds,
the man
           who knew this final curve of land
as home.
They had always known
it was a settlement, a kind of reverence
kept them from building
until the topsoil was stripped.
    Underneath:
           a driftwood fence, thick-walled
                        sod buildings, scattering
                                    of iron nails.
Today a gas-powered fire burns in the pit
at L'Anse aux Meadows,
warming a woman in period garb, gaggle
    of visitors.

    The Vikings would have liked
these restless grasses overlooking the Strait,
sunlight moving across Labrador cliffs.
Heather and berries, twisted hull on a shore.
A freighter passes Quirpon Island,
    the last island in the world.
                        After that
                                    there was only water.

    Thirty-five men and five women—
and the children
would have found partridgeberries, bakeapples,
blueberries, and crowberries, and the red berries
you crack between your teeth for water.
They would have seen
these lichens bursting out of the ground—
cumulous clouds of creamy white
        palest green   eye-searing yellow—
and the woman approaching,
dark-complected and almond-eyed,
pulling handfuls of berries from the bushes
    with a practiced hand.

In the only restaurant at L'Anse aux Meadows,
iceberg ice in our glasses, linen napkins,
a blue sea in the picture window
and a photograph of a coastal steamer: black hull
rising from the ice, bleak headland from the ocean.
People rushing towards it—
dog sleds and derricks,
the boxes of supplies.
It's 1940-something and the road
    will not be built until 1963.

The dogs, they could be stubborn, you know.
They could lie down in the snow and refuse.
They could love this man but not
his brother.
            The brother
tried to drag the lead dog forward
and when she turned and headed home,
he kicked her leg and broke it.
She had to be put down, of course,
and in the midst of winter, ten children to feed,
they could haul neither wood nor water,
nor the seal meat home.

    "I can't say
I remembered it as hard," she said,
"Oh there must have been hardship—
running short of food, making everything,
all your clothes, but we had plenty
of company in each other,
and such dances! My grandfather's accordion,
seventy-five people, chairs pulled back to the wall—
and on stormy days at Christmas
we tasseled the dogs' harnesses with yellow, red, green—
whatever yarn we had."

Then in the spring in Flower's Cove
the ships arrived
and everyone went out to meet them,
boats and people bobbing
where the ice pans had broken up.
You could look back across the water as a child
and all you would see was yellow.
          "That was the buttercups
                    yes, buttercups and dandelions."

          *

    What did the Vikings think
  as they swept down from Labrador,
when they first caught sight of Belle Isle,
          the jewel at the mouth
of the deep-water-fast-current-cobalt-blue straits
  where the calving icebergs were floating south
      and the whales were swimming north
              in the spring
        in the Strait of Belle Isle?

Wednesday

A long road through forests,
a long road, passing empty mobile homes
and occasionally a car.
I am tired,
the driver tires and if it weren't for the fact
there are no other roads to follow
we would wander at this point
and our eyes would close.
It is time to stop for the night
between shadows of moose on the shoulders.
The wind is buffeting the van—
narrow pavement, a strip of gravel,
and now the breakers.
Salt furs the windshield, the headlights blur,
we see almost nothing in the long half light.
    Beloved, what was on the map no longer
has a bearing. We cannot tell
if the road continues on or ends.
We cannot find the places in the guide book.
We hug the road. It hugs us back,
lifeline into Port aux Choix:
cones of streetlights saturated with salt,
spare buildings and a nest of streets.
The only place we see is full,
we cannot understand the accent
        or directions that are offered us—

    We find it finally,
the lightless rattling building on the shore
with pool table, bar, and microwave.
The proprietor limps and searches up and down
to find a teakettle for us.
The place is cheap, the heat
        and TV work.

    Wind is pounding at the door.
It takes all our strength to close and still
some consciousness on the other side
presses with its shoulder.
At last the latch snaps shut and we retire

to the green wallpaper, maroon
comforter, two small photographs—
something touching, that showed some care,
    I can't remember now—
This detour off the poolroom, the neighbours
sway from rooms to cars, the backdoor
    surging like an airlock.

    Oh, it's blowing a bit, they say,
yes, maybe a good gale
on the far end of a point in the North Atlantic.
But the hurricane passed east of here,
its long arms trailing spray, exhausted swimmer
    rising out of the surf.
                She swam

    for thirteen hours. No one heard her cries
above the wind, and the shrimp trawler
continued on and disappeared into the swell.
For a whole night she swam and floated,
floated and swam, heading for a low
recurring sound—fog horn on an oil rig.
She hauled herself up on the platform.
    "I just had to be strong," she said,
I didn't want to go like that, to be eaten by the fishes."

But that was south of here, in a far
    far warmer ocean.

    *

When I looked at a map I saw
we were on an island, or almost an island;
the print obscured the topography
and in the end it didn't matter—
the motel was at the water's edge,
and the Canadian flag was out straight and fraying
    in the sovereign wind
                of Newfoundland.

*

      The Basques, the French, the English:
  no one came here for the land,
though one could fall in love with tundra,
one's heart could be cheered by roadside
gardens webbed with blaze orange,
the parsnips, the globes of cabbages—
Why there of all places? On a highway
off a shoulder too narrow and too steep,
in the woods, no town around
that one could see.

No, the glaciers had worked hard and long
to plow the dirt into the sea,
where the waters were so thick with fish
    you could pull them up in bucketfuls,
                so wrote a 15th century whaler.

   *

[a cove   where people remember
going to the lumber mill by outboard motor. Pickup on a
bluff, man with cigarette & open can. Not old, maybe past
his prime   a total glassy calm
                   yes,   he spent a lot
of hours out there on that water.

     "I never thought I'd see the day when I had to pay a
fine for cod."
        ]

29

Thursday

They had lived here, at Philip's Garden by the sea,
a people who left only tiny ivory
polar bear amulets and soapstone pots.
Now irises cluster
in each foundation's faint depression—
a seething meadow and rolling water.
        They must
have had patience in their bones,
bent over their delicate sawtooth barbs
in this light-struck grass,
opened to the fierce wind and scuttling sky.

        All the points are under glass:
long serrated blades, each tooth
chipped to a deadly edge: harpoon heads,
arrow heads, scrapers and bones,
and a trail
clear across northern Canada, the Strait
    frozen over—

    A backdrop etched with figures
in sepia and ochre, an artist's guess.
Benches and cooking pots, the suggestion
of a drying sealskin,
lodge of skins stretched over a wooden frame.
        A thousand years might come and go unnoticed,
the same universe extended overhead—
Dorset Eskimos, the Groswater people,
they came and then they went,
when famine took them or they had done
    what they had come to do.

        *

We find a fossil in the gravel, tightly coiled
around itself
                and then another
                        and another,
limey pebbles in an expanse of pebbles—

Up to Crow's Head, down
   into licheny pines,
     into the moss and seeping boulders,
    damp path turning tight
  against a damp rock wall,
hidden graves of ancient peoples.

Distant tableau of buildings.
We bend double on this white spit, teeth chattering, wind-
breakers billowing.
      The weather changes
              from inlet to inlet—

              to get out of the belting wind and find
a baker
     radiating warm stickiness of lemon tarts.

    *

    Broom Point:
  breakers and a double rainbow,
four white fishing cottages.
You can see the flowered curtains, potted plant
on a windowsill, a small tight
kitchen table.
Empty home in a row of empty homes—

Someone
moved the people out,
      someone with a vision.
The people packed up
their china and their way of life,
and everyone pretended
there was no one living there.
No schools, no roads to nameless places,
  no headstones
    to mark the dead.

*

It was as if
you were not there but then you were.
You came around a point to find
a few cottages against a bluff,
a life hidden from the outside
unless you had foreknowledge:
you had heard a story or seen a map.
Even now you could drive by
　　　　Barr'd Harbour

　　　　　　　　　　and never notice.

*

The sun goes face first into the spray,
a seagull heads into the wind,
mountains behind us flushed with light.
Rainbow, a rainbow—
everywhere
the sea is beaten with a broom,
　　waves are boiling in a pot.

All our lives the sea has pounded at the door,
until one day you have to go and open up
and let the water in.
You cannot sweep the ocean
from the kitchen with a broom
as my parents tried in the hurricane of '54.
The waters poured down the street,
the boats floated by,
and the raft I swam to as a child
　　went through the picture window in the night.

Friday

Today the sea is benign.
    It is not
as it was one January
gathering its thoughts against the slow, determined ferry
to Port aux Basques,
which rode out the storm in the open ocean
fully loaded. The passengers
had not expected to spend the night
out there in the heaving water.
            They had hotel reservations
or family waiting, or a quiet room with a light
    and a table, a book and a chair
                            and perhaps a cat.
But there they were.

    But we
have a southwest breeze, a sky
one could fall into—blue pool, blue eye—
steep meadow dropping off to the sea.
A butterfly spreads its wings
in the thistles and purple asters.

Today
    we walked without looking, thinking our feet
would find their blind way through the fields
    of peridotite boulders.
        Our feet took us
            down the forested slope to where the sheep
    wander up and down.
The sheep are here to examine the sea stacks,
the sheep trace the earth's mantle to the Moho.
We follow their paths into the tuckamore,
    safe from the wind,
        the three-foot-high
    arching branchways and spangly boughs,
        a place to make a home if the three-inch mat
            of wool is not enough.
One could crawl into the greeny thickets and hide,
away from all the others,
    while the sun went on making the day outside.

One could do this and not be missed
　　and not miss
　　the ocean's wild assault on the headlands—
　sea caves pounding far below with immense
basaltic hearts—
nor the blue air and promise of joyfulness,
while one dreamed
of daily chewable grass, took on a sheep's hide
　　and sheep's mind:
　　　stolid, unthoughtful, and satisfied.

　　　*

　A campground
with an empty ranger station,
weather forecast from two days ago
　　　and us
driving round unable to decide
which site to take or whether there's a reason why
there is no one else besides us.
　Ice is spreading down from Labrador.
The people who do not belong
have fewer places they can hide.
The people who do not belong
　are moving south to land's end,
　　　　　　　the ferry terminal.

　　*

　　Later
　　　　we both would think of Casablanca　　*the fog*
in the darkness turned everything gray & grainy　*dark wood*
of the hotel, sweeping stairway to the second floor

　Something about an outpost
　　　　　　　& all the guests departing by ferry

40

Saturday

Last night a man from North Carolina was at Eileen's.
He had just gotten off the Labrador ferry
after walking the streets of Nain.
A person could go all the way to Hebron,
a name on the map where you find
an empty Moravian church on a bluff,
knurled turrets and wooden frame,
     a yellow sky and distant sun.

     I am only describing what I have seen
on the cover of a brochure,
landscapes of ethereal light,
the scrunch of gritty stone underfoot,
     shimmering scrim of pink and green.
          You could go there if you wanted to badly enough
     as this man did
from Cartwright and Goose Bay
to Makkovik, Postville, Davis Inlet, and Nain.
You could see the labradorite for yourself,
slabs of iridescent bacon in the bedrock, the same
perfect angularity of the mountains
     only greener, bluer, a pale
                         cold light—

     One could think of angels, not the kind
that come to comfort but the kind
that hold over you the sum total of your days
and ask for an accounting:
the sword bearers, standard bearers,
those who throw the salmon on the scales
to parcel out what belongs to him
and what to her,
so the final account be closed,
          the books be shut,
                         and let the snows begin.

*

All afternoon we watched as others climbed
the scree-filled slash in the mountainside.
Pink Shirt & Black Hat
are almost to the top, four Blue Shirts
founder at the narrow point. From the base
of Gros Morne we get a fix
on them through binoculars,
clambering over boulders—weigh
the wisdom of gambling our bones
                    for the summit of a mountain.

    In the foreground
a black body lurches from the weeds,
moose with dreadlocks and solar collector antlers.
He shakes his head, paws the ground,
we hear a gurgling sound
as he wades into the pond lined with flat
    white stones.

    Late in the day we start up in reverse,
the long way around, seven miles on shifting stones
which will get you to the top
            if you are stubborn,
to the place of arctic hare and caribou,
the looking down instead of looking up.
    We've seen the pictures.
    We've heard people talk about it.

    A man rounds the bend
bare-kneed, bare-chested, muscles and frame
pack bulging: air mattress, sleeping bag, tent,
water bottles dangling. He's just a kid,
tall, gangling,
sweating from stone to stone.
"How's it going?" we ask.
"How much further is it?" he replies,
a question we can't answer.

There's a whiff of uneasiness
as he passes, maybe aching
                so early in the trail, and dusk approaching.
        *

A backward glance:
    an empty space where the moose had been.
Female browses in the brush,
eight turquoise ponds—the eyes of a spider—
clear to the west, clear to the east, and clouds
                blow north to south directly overhead.

Two moose, both female, are gazing at the sea

                        [& all you would see was yellow.]

A backward glance:
    This is the way we boarded the ferry
lest our old lives vanish
and the new world prove to be too much.
Everyone backed on,
    RVs and tractor trailers
moving up the ramp in hesitant starts, the jumpsuited
workers who took the wheel of a forty-foot
luxury apartment to cram
it into the open stern
    of the *Caribou.*

Four lanes of traffic backing into a highway tunnel,
halting in carbon monoxide vapor....

But I knew nothing then
of how things were supposed to be—
uphill and backwards, oh yes.

        *

        Each step jars the bones,
this foot, that boulder,
bone and rock loosely joined

by the cushioning flesh.
We stop—Old Crow across the gulch—
lose ourselves
    in rock and sunlight.

    Years ago
I laced on a brand-new pair of hiking boots
thinking of the peaks I would ascend
and the miles I would put behind me.
Now everything ends at the ocean
    whichever direction I take.
The way home is straight on through
    a gaping
          metallic jaw.

Once a ferry left the dock with the visor
partly open, some water got in.
They had to work to get it closed
    out there in the harbour, and in the end
  no harm came of it.
The ferry continued six hours across the water and then
  went in for repairs.

    Back and forth like the tide
the ferries go.

     *

We are sitting on a rock,
part way up the long way around,
still sitting and the sun is going down.

There are times when it is sufficient
to be where you are.
It is enough to be yourself.

Sunday

CONDITIONS

"...not...liable for personal injury...death, delay, loss of or damage to personal goods... whatever might have been the cause...whether...the fault or neglect of the carrier or of any of the employees or the representatives, the defective condition of the vessel or of any of its rigging, machinery, equipment and appurtenances; acts of God, perils of the sea, fire, explosions on shipboard or elsewhere, labour disturbances, collisions, stranding...fault, negligence or error...in the management or navigation of the vessel or unseaworthiness."

On the third try we get a place on the squat
top-heavy boat, a hundred of us
sliding across a white-capped bay.
We roll and wallow, the water
bunches in hills and hollows.
Cliffs swoop upwards,
a rush of rock cutting the sky like a blade.
The landscape   sways towards us
    then swings back—
we have taken off and are banking
                over deeper water than you would guess.

    Around a bend
the boathouse vanishes, our old life disappears.
Around a bend and then another:
zigzagging fjord, arm of ice.
The ice is to blame—
it squeezed the rocks, it ripped them open.
It soldered the mountains together leaving
the drippy weeping joints.
The ice could burn a place in a person's heart.

49

On the mantelpiece she
kept a picture of Flower's Cove—
bay of ice, scattered houses,
the lighthouse on the point
white on white,
coastal plain without a mountain:
   so beloved
         and monotone.

    *

to keep supple

           sealskin boots stored in the refrigerator, small
rounded feet puckered with careful stitches
waterproof   snowfoot   *centuries & centuries*

    *

We come up short
against a cliff, a gray dock
dips into the water at the end, and a trail
ascends to the lip, continues on
unmarked
through lichen and "wind exposed mats
of black crowberry."
   The path is there
for those who look for it.
Hikers backpack all the way
from Western Brook Pond to Gros Morne Mountain,
looking back at the same breathtaking view
in so many photographs,
back
over cloud and fjord and ridge,
   the sea

                 of buttercups
forever and forever—

*

Water devils course across the pond.

A person could accept the lack of footing,
        the way
the boat yaws with every wave, the foaming chop
    and the depths below.
        The boat becomes
    your life and your salvation.
These are the conditions that are served you—
whatever happens the Lord be with you,
    whatever happens we are wallowing home
                        drunk beyond all hope
    clinging to the slippery fiberglass,
us and thirty others on the upper deck.
Musak playing songs of Newfoundland
drifts in and out with each plunge;
and across the gulf
the dock and boathouse mark the border
    of another nation.

    Beloved, the world is out of our control.
The wind blows to a distant shore always
on the horizon
studded with unknown houses,
boats and stones,
    to pull up in the harbour of a windswept place,
        the new
    found land
finally coming into focus.

    *

        And when you looked back   across the water
all there would be was yellow
            (yes,

                buttercups & dandelions)

Monday

There was a time when holidays were holy,
when people left their oxen and their plows
to journey to Jerusalem, Rome, or Santiago de Compostela.
I have seen   contemporary accounts
of the feasting on the way.
I have seen the guidebooks
advising travelers of the sights, the inns
that grant safe sleep and ones
to be avoided.
        Such travels might leave a person changed
                    and we too

*were homesick and enraptured
sitting by a lake where the landscape
had overtaken us. The sweep of valleys
pulled its scrim across our eyes,
lines of polar magnetism that tugged
at our emotions and defied direction.
        A person
might wander further north
than they intended, see things
        they had not seen before.*

        *

*The caribou's fur
was sable and sand,
a rack of curving antler, and the distant boat tour
drew a long silver V in the water.
On the far side a blue wall
of an opposing mountain rose.*

        *

    If you crack open a stone from the Tablelands
you find the blackest deepest green inside—
glistening intestines of the world,
what came from below the surface below the bedrock
below the crust,

down where rock moves away
from its reassuring hardness
to a languorousness
          that flows a little
                    when pressed.

          I pick up a stone
with an oily darkness and glints of pyroxenes:
a copper-gold-brass-bronze shining,
subterranean heat smoothed and crushed
     until it took the shape of something
          closer to the surface,
               this heaviness
                    I hold.

          *

     On the south side of the lake
a mountain moves into light.
You can see a stippling of trees,
you can see the cut of a rock slide.
What was unknown takes on form,
a coast out on the Atlantic appears
as a dim line and then
          becomes close and familiar:
     dark beach strewn with words and pebbles,
and small gray birds cutting the dusk with their wings.

A person could row
towards some unknown point
without really knowing where it was,
or how to take one's bearings as the Vikings did,
     using wooden instruments to find the polestar
          and discover how far off course they had wandered.
          You might never have been trained
in such ancient arts, or even in the way
to row a dory: with your back to your destination,
          navigating by landmarks you left behind.
          So you might row to exhaustion
knowing you had to cross
     some terrifying space which lay between
          where you were
and where you wanted to be.

Why else would someone set out
on the open ocean in an open boat?

   *

I am stretched out on a rock,
lapped by rippling sun.
Light is flesh, my shirt
    of stones and hope—

A haze gathers at the summit
more than the fuzziness of half-closed eyes.
Clouds move in, somewhere
a ferry slides out of the fog. It is
  the end of summer.

   *

Afterwards I could not remember
what the land was trying to say
or my heart was trying to hear—
  It was something to do
with the white ruff of fur around the caribou's neck
and the slow pace of grazing,
the watchful gaze in our direction, then careful
  moving away.

NOTES

pg 2: So wrote the Vikings a thousand years ago.

pg 5: *bottomer:* a plain round cake

pg 6: Bjarni Herjolfsson was on his way to join Leif Erikson, who had settled in Greenland.

pg 7: Green Point is an international geologic benchmark marking the boundary between the Cambrian and Ordovician periods, the era between spineless creatures and those with proto-backbones.

pg 22: "Losing your lead dog was like losing your car," recounted Eileen Janes, who grew up in the landlocked community of Flower's Cove in the 1940s. A family without the dogs had no way to transport food, water, or wood for heat. A person who became seriously ill in winter was taken by dogsled some eighty kilometers to the medical facility at St. Anthony.

pg 28: In 2003, Melinda Lopez was rescued having swum all night after falling off a shrimp trawler in the Gulf of Mexico.

pg 28: Promised food and health care, Newfoundland joined the Canadian federation under economic duress. Martin Janes, a retired history teacher, commented that "Newfoundland was the only country in the world to have voted itself out of existence."

pg 34: The fishing cottages at Broom Point are currently a display at Gros Morne National Park. Historically, English settlements dotted this shore owned by the French, but even the government in St. John's refused to recognize their existence. The outports did not appear on maps, were ineligible for aid, and were officially invisible.

pg 49: The quote is taken from the ticket stub of a local tour boat.

pp 49 & 50: Western Brook Pond is a seven-mile-long fjord of considerable depth.

ACKNOWLEGEMENTS

Thanks to the editor of *The Northern Raven* in which three sections first appeared in an earlier form. Thanks also to Donna Francis and the staff of Creative Book Publishing; to Mark Callanan for his thoughtful and sharp-eyed editing; to Stephen Schmidt for the cover photograph of Partridgeberry Hill in Woody Point; Rosemary Johnson for her continued encouragement; to Dara Wier, Abbot Cutler, Janine Roberts, Susan Middleton, Wally Swist, and Dorothy McFarland for their criticism and suggestions on earlier drafts; and as always, to Steve, for sharing this voyage with me.

Special thanks are due to Martin and Eileen Janes for sharing their knowledge and stories of Newfoundland, which gave me insight into the island I would never have had otherwise. I am especially thankful to Eileen for sharing her stories of growing up in a landlocked community on the Great Northern Peninsula; and especially indebted to Martin for much of what I now know about Newfoundland history. To both, I thank them for their patience in answering my many questions.